Kath Walker

THE DAWN IS AT HAND

Selected Poems

Introduction by Malcolm Williamson
Master of the Queen's Music

Marion Boyars
London · New York

First published in Great Britain and the United States in 1992
by Marion Boyars Publishers
24 Lacy Road, London SW15 1NL
237 East 39th Street, New York, N.Y. 10016

First published in Australia for the
Australian market only in 1970 by
Jacaranda Press under the title *My People*.

British Library Cataloguing in Publication Data
Walker, Kath, *1920–*
   The dawn is at hand.
   I. Title
   821

Library of Congress Cataloging in Publication Data
Walker, Kath, 1920–
   The dawn is at hand : selected poems / by Kath Walker:
introduction by Malcolm Williamson.
   Earlier ed. published under title: My people. 1970. (Australia
only)
   1. Australian aborigines—Poetry. I. Walker, Kath, 1920– My
people. II. Title.
   PR9619.3.W24D38   1992
   821—dc20   91–23568

ISBN 0–7145–2921–4 Original Paperback

Typeset by Ann Buchan (Typesetters) in 11½/13½ Baskerville and Optima
Printed in Great Britain by Itchen Printers, Southampton

CONTENTS

Malcolm Williamson's Choral Symphony *The Dawn is at Hand*, based on Kath Walker's poems, was published in 1989 by Campion Press, Buntingford, Hertfordshire SG9 0QW, England, to whom applications for scores and performance rights should be made.

INTRODUCTION

How old is space? Where is time? How young is democracy? Who better than the Australian Aboriginal people know? Before Abraham was, Australians in their tribal cities understood. Their happy liaison with Mother Earth enabled them to know what was to be known, to accept what was and is mystery.

After the unbroken nomadic democracies of near enough 100,000 years lived in the reflection of their eternity, the Dreaming, there came, a mere two centuries ago, a crude and cruel eruption for which ignorance alone can be blamed. The infant civilization of Europe bore south to lasso what was imagined to be a vast and vacant continent. Innocence was lost. Coffin ships came bearing gifts of alcohol, lying and disease hitherto undreamed of in the Dreaming.

The Aborigines gazed on the white interlopers in wonder; the Europeans responded with aggression traditional to their survival culture.

Mystifyingly, two centuries later, white supremacy and near eradication of the world's oldest extant culture are celebrated. A wiser age, still awaited, might have attempted a pluralistic culture and ethnicity. One such culture could have tilted the world on its axis. It is the eleventh hour and, as with Faust, salvation is just possible.

Contemporary Australia is a thrilling hotchpotch of excellence and mediocrity — at once wiser and less wise than any other nation in our world. The burden of needful redemption rests on a pathetically few shoulders. For all its tiny population pitted against diversity in vastness Australia has thrown up more than its share of philosopher-rulers. Too often unheeded because of their improbability and threatened with scything, reluctant politicians and inconvenient artists have stood tall. One such is Kath Walker, born 1920, an Aboriginal poet, survivor of blood sacrifice and prophet of wise hope, master of outrageous hyperbole and intuitive Socratic disciple.

In 1987, I was offered several commissions to write works for the Australian Bicentenary of 1988 designed to celebrate the white man's incursion into the Australian Continent. I had decided to reject one such offer since it came from Queensland because of its unappealing history of injustice to the Aboriginal people. I met a representative of the commissioning body in Sydney. I had prepared my lordly, disdainful rejection of the offer. 1988 seemed to me a year when sorrow for man's inhumanity to man would have been more suitable than celebration of white conquest. Leaving me no chance to accept or reject the offer, I was asked 'Had you thought about setting Kath Walker to music?' I knew and admired her poems and, without allowing more than a second for astonishment, I shook his hand and said, 'Done!' He explained that the great lady had never allowed her poems to be set to music and that, therefore, two trials had to be undergone to gain her permission — the first, by telephone; the second, face to face.

The long-distance telephone call, deeply serious but laced with laughter, was the first trial. What did I think of Margaret Thatcher, of Ronald Reagan, of the Premier of Queensland? Almost as directly, probing questions about Love, Sexuality, Justice, Retribution, Forgiveness. The first trial led to an invitation to visit.

I flew to Brisbane and then, with two musical colleagues, took the ferry over what might be thought of as Kath Walker's ocean to Stradbroke Island. We drove the dusty roads through the lush and lusty tropical vegetation to a cluster of tents and caravans among the trees. It was nationally known that Kath's home had been vandalized and, since the Queensland police had declined to investigate the matter and no compensation was forthcoming, the Walker family preferred to live on common land in the traditional 'sitting-down place' of the

Noonuccal tribe in circumstances precluding a recurrence of the injustice.

A small, dainty woman, elegant in a cerise dress and hat which would command admiration in any fashionable street in the world, came to greet us. Embraces seemed entirely natural. Although photographs had made the face familiar, nothing prepared us for the beautiful aquamarine eyes that bespeak innocence, intelligence and wisdom. Kath led us to the veranda and offered us cucumber sandwiches, tropical fruit and tea. In a clearing nearby was a fire of wood and stones being heated for their evening barbecue.

Although time seemed to have stopped, none was wasted in preliminaries. We realized that we had the total acceptance of a loving, candid and indomitable woman. Like Jonathan Jo, she has a wheelbarrow full of surprises. Her strikingly beautiful hands, marvellously manicured and beringed are never without a cigarette. As she waved one towards the distant roadway she shouted, 'I'll stop smoking when people stop driving cars.' Through the sunlit hours when we were together we submitted to the paradoxical delights of the mercurial personality of a poet who would recite poems, mostly not her own but which she admired, interposed with amusing bawdy anecdotes, mercilessly accurate denunciations of those who deserved them and unstinted selfless praise of such colleagues as the historian Manning Clark and the great poet Judith Wright.

Essentially every poem, like every spontaneous remark whether literal or metaphorical, is pumiced to shining meaning. The gear-box has yet to be developed which can change gear as Kath's mind does and only indicative fragments can be reproduced here. While she was recounting the story of her trip as a delegate to the People's Republic of China I was removing the teacups. Kath looked over her shoulder to the kitchen and said, 'Your Mother brought you up well, Malcolm', and continued to talk about China. Having studied all her printed poems, so diverse and rich, I had arrived with the list in sequence of the poems I wanted to set for what was to become the hour-long choral symphony *The Dawn is at Hand*. In a rapid switch from reciting a poem by the West Australian Aboriginal poet Jack Davis whom she greatly admires, Kath look my list and, giving sound reasons, reassembled it adding some poems, taking others away. It is hard to know how, before any music was written, she had so astutely envisaged the structure which stands so satisfactorily as the final text.

Thus the second trial was passed. Reluctantly, as a bottle of port was produced and the beef was set for barbecue, we left, laden with passion fruit.

As I went to work on my music, my excitement about the poetry was intensified by the aura of the poet, but simultaneously burdened by the responsibility of looking greatness in the face.

My next meeting with Kath was at as memorable a theatrical evening as I have ever experienced — an Aboriginal manifestation in Sydney written, directed, lit and choreographed by her brilliant son, Vivian. Kath was in the cast as singer, dancer and reciter. She was, at the time, 67 years old but in every department showed the effortless grace of a teenager.

At the first performance of *The Dawn is at Hand* to a crowded house in Brisbane Concert Hall with the full panoply of soloists, chorus and orchestra Kath and I unwittingly made history. Never before had an Aboriginal poet and a Caucasian composer collaborated in so vast a work. We stood together holding hands in the royal box to acknowledge deafening applause which seemed to last almost the length of the work and for scheduling reasons was eventually curtailed by the national radio. It was shortly after this that the overtly racist government of Queensland, which had for so long been a scarcely concealed scandal, fell.

Kath Walker, poet, essayist, painter, actress and

dancer regards herself principally as an educator and, to date, in her Stradbroke Island school well over 30,000 children have passed through her hands. She is, so far, the recipient of honorary doctorates in three Australian states. She has been awarded the M.B.E. for her services to literature and the list of international honours from five continents would occupy pages. A pacifist in life, she is a fighter with the pen. While she and her poems have been chosen to represent Australian literature in North America, Eastern and Western Europe, the Republics of Africa and Asia including China, while every Australian schoolchild knows *We are Going* and *Song of Hope* she has suffered enough personal humiliations in her native Queensland to quench a lesser spirit. However, as we may read in her poem *Let us not be bitter*, it is characteristic of Kath to have compassion for her detractors; but woe betide anybody imprudent enough to open battle with that sharp intellect and flashing tongue, as I know to my personal cost. Although we neither of us knew it, we were both in Moscow at the time of Glasnost:

Kath: 'Why didn't you come to hear me read?'

Me: 'I was at the Soviet Composers' Union.'

Kath: 'Well, that was your bad luck, wasn't it?'

There is every reason to believe that posterity will place Kath Walker as one of the leading poets of our time. Her poetry speaks for itself but, leaving aside the extraordinary gift, the historical and cultural confluences were unforeseeable and unrepeatable. A small girl of some Scottish, some Spanish and much Aboriginal blood had, on the one hand, rudimentary European education imposed on her, while converging with the meditative study of Biami, the indefinable god of creation. The young culture of Europe and the world's oldest culture were absorbed side by side thus forging a unique poetic voice. To date, some 350 Aboriginal root languages have been codified. An Aboriginal poet, Kevin Gilbert, has collected much poetry in these tribal languages like Kath's own Noonuccal, but she has elected to speak her message in English.

Theses on her work abound. What is more significant is that had history been different, had Caucasians occupied Australia for 100,000 years and had Aboriginal aggressors arrived two centuries ago, Kath Walker would have been the champion of the persecuted white people. I can claim no originality for this thought. It has been voiced by American Indians, by Inuits, by persecuted Africans and, indeed, by victims of injustice the world over who refuse to abandon hope and dignity.

Dedicated to the many people,
both black and white,
who are fighting for a Makarrata
(Aboriginal land treaty)
and
to my son Kabul
of the tribe Noonuccal
Custodian of the land Minjerribah
(Vivian Charles Walker)

ALL ONE RACE

Black tribe, yellow tribe, red, white or brown,
From where the sun jumps up to where it goes down,
Herrs and pukka-sahibs, demoiselles and squaws,
All one family, so why make wars?
They're not interested in brumby runs,
We don't hanker after Midnight Suns;
I'm for all humankind, not colour gibes;
I'm international, and never mind tribes.

Black, white or brown race, yellow race or red,
From the torrid equator to the ice-fields spread,
Monsieurs and senors, lubras and fraus,
All one family, so why family rows?
We're not interested in their igloos,
They're not mad about kangaroos;
I'm international, never mind place;
I'm for humanity, all one race.

Away with bitterness, my own dark people
Come stand with me, look forward, not back,
For a new time has come for us.
Now we must change, my people. For so long
Time for us stood still; now we know
Life is change, life is progress,
Life is learning things, life is onward.
White men had to learn civilized ways,
Now it is our turn.
Away with bitterness and the bitter past;
Let us try to understand the white man's ways
And accept them as they accept us;
Let us judge white people by the best of their race.
The prejudiced ones are less than we,
We want them no more than they want us.
Let us not be bitter, that is an empty thing,
A maggot in the mind.
The past is gone like our childhood days of old,
The future comes like dawn after the dark,
Bringing fulfilment.

AN APPEAL

Statesmen, who make the nation's laws,
With power to force unfriendly doors,
Give leadership in this our cause
    That leaders owe.

Writers, who have the nation's ear,
Your pen a sword opponents fear,
Speak of our evils loud and clear
    That all may know.

Unions, who serve democracy,
Guardians of social liberty,
Warm to the justice of our plea,
    And strike your blow.

Churches, who preach the Nazarene,
Be on our side and intervene,
Show us what Christian love can mean
    Who need it so.

The Press, most powerful of all,
On you the underprivileged call:
Right us a wrong and break the thrall
    That keeps us low.

All white well-wishes, in the end
On you our chiefest hopes depend;
Public opinion's our best friend
    To beat the foe.

Three nights they heard the curlew cry.
It is the warning known of old
That tells them one tonight shall die.

Brother and friend, he comes and goes
Out of the Shadow Land to them,
The loneliest voice that earth knows.

He guards the welfare of his own,
He comes to lead each soul away —
To what dim world, what strange unknown?

Who is it that tonight must go:
The old blind one? The cripple child?
Tomorrow all the camp will know.

The poor dead will be less afraid,
Their tribe brother will be with him
When the dread journey must be made.

'Have courage, death is not an end,'
He seems to say. 'Though you must weep,
Death is kindly and is your friend.'

Three nights the curlew cried. Once more
He comes to take the timorous dead —
To what grim change, what ghostly shore?

Note: The curlew was brother of the Aborigines. He came to warn them of a coming death by crying near a camp three nights in succession. They believed that the curlew came to lead the shade of the dead one away to the unknown world.

Something obscene
In man-made sounds affronts the sweet and clean,
But Nature's never.
Shout of the stormy winds, ever
Toneless and rude, tossing the trees,
The harsh scream of seabirds — these
Somehow belong
As much as the wren's airy song.
Man only, the books tell, knows evil and wrong;
Even as art now the yelp and yell
Like music of hell,
Music made evil, the squawk and squall
When the disc jockeys loose the blare and bawl.
Give me the sounds God made so —
I love them all
Whether loud or low,
From the small, thin
Note of the bee's violin
To the rough sea's uproar,
In wild tumult tumbling upon the shore.

TREE GRAVE

When our lost one left us
For the Shadow Land,
In bark we bound him,
A weeping band,
And we bore him, wailing
Our wild death croon
To his lonely tree-grave
By the Long Lagoon.

Our wandering fires
Are now far away,
But our thoughts are turning
By night and day
Where he lies for ever
Under the white moon,
By the lit waters
Of the still lagoon.

His hunts are over
And the songs he made;
Poor lonely fellow,
He will be afraid
When the night winds whisper
Their ghostly tune
In the haunted swamp-oaks
By the Long Lagoon.

Dim light of daybreak now
Faintly over the sleeping camp.
Old lubra first to wake remembers:
First thing every dawn
Remember the dead, cry for them.
Softly at first her wail begins,
One by one as they wake and hear
Join in the cry, and the whole camp
Wails for the dead, the poor dead
Gone from here to the Dark Place:
They are remembered.
Then it is over, life now,
Fires lit, laughter now,
And a new day calling.

All about the country,
From earliest teens,
Dark unmarried mothers,
Fair game for lechers —
Bosses and station hands,
And in town and city
Low-grade animals
Prowl for safe prey.
Nothing done about it,
No one to protect them —
But hush, you mustn't say so,
Bad taste or something
To challenge the accepted,
Disturbing the established.
Turn the blind eye,
Wash the hands like Pilate.

Consent? Even with consent
It is still seduction.
Is it a white girl?
Then court case and headline
Stern talk of maintenance.
Is it a dark girl?
Then safe immunity;
He takes what he wants

And walks off like a dog.
Was ever even one,
One of all the thousands
Ever made responsible?
For dark unmarried mothers
The law does not run.
No blame for the guilty
But blame uttered only
For anyone made angry
Who dares even mention it,
Challenging old usage,
Established, accepted
And therefore condoned.
Shrug away the problem,
The shame, the injustice;
Turn the blind eye,
Wash the hands like Pilate.

NOT MY STYLE

Not my style?
Man! the world will end
And you complain.
I want to do
The things I have not done.
Not just taste the nectar of Gods
But drown in it too.
Shed my grass-root skin.
Emerge!
As woman!
   poet!
      writer!
         musician!

Eat herbs;
Chew grass;
Commit suicide;
Live.
Stuff myself
Of the bitter and the sweet,
Before,
   that thing,
      that thing,
        outside
Comes.

Change is the law. The new must oust the old.
I look at you and am back in the long ago,
Old pinnaroo lonely and lost here,
Last of your clan.
Left only with your memories, you sit
And think of the gay throng, the happy people,
The voices and the laughter
All gone, all gone,
And you remain alone.

I asked and you let me hear
The soft vowelly tongue to be heard now
No more for ever. For me
You enact old scenes, old ways, you who have used
Boomerang and spear.
You singer of ancient tribal songs,
You leader once in the corroboree,
You twice in fierce tribal fights
With wild enemy blacks from over the river,
All gone, all gone. And I feel
The sudden sting of tears, Willie Mackenzie

In the Salvation Army Home.
Displaced person in your own country,
Lonely in teeming city crowds,
Last of your tribe.

Note: Willie Mackenzie was a full-blood Aboriginal, the last surviving member of the Darwarbada tribe of the Caboolture district. He died in 1968, age unknown but probably in the eighties. His tribal name was Geerbo, his totem the native bee. The 'Mackenzie' came from his family's first white boss, a selector of that name.

THE CHILD WIFE

They gave me to an old man,
Joyless and old,
Life's smile of promise
So soon to frown.
Inside his gunya
My childhood over,
I must sit for ever,
And the tears fall down.

It was love I longed for,
Young love like mine,
It was Dunwa wanted me,
The gay and brown.
Oh, old laws that tether me!
Oh, long years awaiting me!
And the grief comes over me,
And the tears fall down.

Happy the small birds
Mating and nesting,
Shrilling their gladness
No grief may drown.
But an old man's gunya
Is my life for ever,
And I think of Dunwa,
And the tears fall down.

Crooning her own girl thoughts and dreams
The young girl Wanda,
Grinding nardoo with the women
Softly chanted her simple song
Of all she hated.

'I hate death and the going away,
All sad endings.
I hate things that have no joy,'
Said the young girl Wanda.
'I hate sunset bringing the dark
That is full of secrets,
I hate silence of desolate places,
Swamp-oaks sighing by lonely waters,
And tree graves,'
Said the young girl Wanda.
'I hate old men's rules and laws,
Old wrinkled faces,
The elders who no longer know
What the young know,'
Said the young girl Wanda.

'All time too much hate, you,'
Said the old gin Onah.
'Tell us what you love.'

'I love joy of life,
I love arms around me,
I love life and love,'
Said the young girl Wanda.
'I love all young things,
The young dawn, not the grey day dying,
The white of daybreak on awaking waters.
I love happy things,'
Said the young girl Wanda.
'High eagles, the light in eyes we love,
The camp crying for joy when one returns.
I love colour, berries yellow and red,
The grass when it is green,
The blue that is on the kingfisher,
And a bright flower for my black hair,'
Said the young girl Wanda,
'But most of all my strong lover I love,
And his arms under me.'

Officiously they hawked about
'Petition' to keep abos out,
And slavishly, without a peep,
The feeble yes-men signed like sheep.

And are we still the ousted, then,
And dare you speak for decent men?
This site was ours, you may recall,
Ages before you came at all.

'No abos here!' Why not, Whynot?
And if black-balling and boycott,
First black-ball pride and arrogance,
Boycott this vile intolerance.

Since God's good world began,
Not God but godless man
Made barrier and ban,
   And reared each frontier wall.
Brothers, when shall we see
Selfless democracy?
Life is for liberty,
   And earth was made for all.

Let little kiplings rant,
Narrow and arrogant,
Their chauvinistic cant
   That white is nobler birth.
The best of every race
Should here find welcome place;
The colour of his face
   Is no man's test of worth.

White men, turn quickly the earth of Acacia Ridge,
Hide the evidence lying there
Of the black race evicted
        as of old their fathers were;
Cover up the crime committed this day,
Call it progress, the white man's way.

Take no heed of the pregnant
        black woman in despair
As with her children she has to go;
Ignore her bitter tears that unheeded flow;
While her children cling to her terrified
Bulldozers huddle the crime aside.

White men, turn quickly the earth of Acacia Ridge,
Plough the guilt in, cover and hide the shame;
These are black and so without right to blame
As bulldozers brutally drive, ruthless and sure
Through and over the poor homes
        of the evicted poor.

Homeless now they stand
        and watch as the rain pours down;

This is the justice brought to the black man there,
Injustice which to whites you would never dare,
You whites with all the power and privilege
Who committed the crime of Acacia Ridge.

THE UNHAPPY RACE
The Myall Speaks

White fellow, you are the unhappy race.
You alone have left nature
        and made civilized laws.
You have enslaved yourselves as you enslaved
        the horse and other wild things.
Why, white man?
Your police lock up your tribe in houses with bars,
We see poor women scrubbing floors
        of richer women.
Why, white man, why?
You laugh at 'poor blackfellow',
        you say we must be like you.
You say we must leave the old freedom and leisure,
We must be civilized and work for you.
Why, white fellow?
Leave us alone, we don't want
        your collars and ties,
We don't need your routines and compulsions.
We want the old freedom
        and joy that all things have but you,
Poor white man of the unhappy race.

CORROBOREE

Hot day dies, cook time comes.
Now between the sunset and the sleep-time
Time of playabout.
The hunters paint black bodies
       by firelight with designs of meaning
To dance corroboree.
Now didgeridoo compels with
       haunting drone eager feet to stamp,
Click-sticks click in rhythm to swaying bodies
Dancing corroboree.
Like spirit things in from
       the great surrounding dark
Ghost-gums dimly seen stand at the edge of light
Watching corroboree.
Eerie the scene in leaping firelight,
Eerie the sounds in that wild setting,
As naked dancers weave stories of the tribe
Into corroboree.

STONE AGE

White man, only time is between us.
Once in the time long gone you lived in caves,
You used stone axe, you clothed yourself in skins,
You too feared the dark, fled the unknown.
Go back, remember your own Alcheringa
When lightning still was magic and you hid
From terrible thunder rolling in the sky.
White superior race, only time is between us —
As some are grown up and others yet children.
We are the last of the Stone Age tribes,
Waiting for time to help us
As time helped you.

Pour your pitcher of wine into the wide river
And where is your wine? There is only the river.
Must the genius of an old race die
That the race might live?
We who would be one with you, one people,
We must surrender now much that we love,
The old freedoms for new musts,
Your world for ours,
But a core is left that we must keep always.
Change and compel, slash us into shape,
But not our roots deep in the soil of old.
We are different hearts and minds
In a different body. Do not ask of us
To be deserters, to disown our mother,
To change the unchangeable.
The gum cannot be trained into an oak.
Something is gone, something surrendered, still
We will go forward and learn.
Not swamped and lost, watered away, but keeping
Our own identity, our pride of race.
Pour your pitcher of wine into the wide river
And where is your wine? There is only the river.

INTEGRATION — YES!

Gratefully we learn from you,
The advanced race,
You with long centuries of lore behind you.
We who were Australians long before
You who came yesterday,
Eagerly we must learn to change,
Learn new needs we never wanted,
New compulsions never needed,
The price of survival.
Much that we loved is gone and had to go,
But not the deep indigenous things.
The past is still so much a part of us,
Still about us, still within us.
We are happiest
Among our own people. We would like to see
Our own customs kept, our old
Dances and songs, crafts and corroborees.
Why change our sacred myths
           for your sacred myths?
No, not assimilation but integration,
Not submergence but our uplifting,
So black and white may go forward together
In harmony and brotherhood.

My father was Noonuccal man and
    kept old tribal way,
His totem was the Carpet Snake,
    whom none must ever slay;
But mother was of Peewee clan,
    and loudly she expressed
The daring view that carpet snakes
    were nothing but a pest.

Now one lived right inside with us
    in full immunity,
For no one dared to interfere
    with father's stern decree:
A mighty fellow ten feet long,
    and as we lay in bed
We kids could watch him round a beam
    not far above our head.

Only the dog was scared of him,
    we'd hear its whines and growls,
But mother fiercely hated him
    because he took her fowls.
You should have heard her diatribes
    that flowed in angry torrents
With words you never see in print,
    except in D.H. Lawrence.

'I kill that robber,' she would scream,
   fierce as a spotted cat;
'You see that bulge inside of him?
    My speckly hen make that!'
But father's loud and strict command
   made even mother quake;
I think he'd sooner kill a man
   than kill a carpet snake.

That reptile was a greedy-guts,
   and as each bulge digested
He'd come down on the hunt at night
   as appetite suggested.
We heard his stealthy slithering sound
   across the earthen floor,
While the dog gave a startled yelp
   and bolted out the door.

Then over in the chicken-yard
   hysterical fowls gave tongue,
Loud frantic squawks accompanied by
   the barking of the mung,
Until at last the racket passed,
   and then to solve the riddle,

Next morning he was back up there
        with a new bulge in his middle.

When father died we wailed and cried,
        our grief was deep and sore;
And strange to say from that sad day
        the snake was seen no more.
The wise old men explained to us:
        'It was his tribal brother,
And that is why it done a guy' —
        but some looked hard at mother.

She seemed to have a secret smile,
        her eyes were smug and wary,
She looked as innocent as the cat
        that ate the pet canary.
We never knew, but anyhow
        (to end this tragic rhyme)
I think we all had snake for tea
        one day about that time.

THE TEACHERS

For Mother who was never taught to read or write

Holy men, you came to preach:
'Poor black heathen, we will teach
Sense of sin and fear of hell,
Fear of God and boss as well;
We will teach you work for play,
We will teach you to obey
Laws of God and laws of Mammon. . .'
And we answered, 'No more gammon,
If you have to teach the light,
Teach us first to read and write.'

WHITE MAN

Abo man, we
To you have brought
Our social science,
And you we have taught
Our white democracy.

DARK MAN

White man, who
Would teach us and tame,
We had socialism
Long before you came,
And democracy too.

WHITE MAN

Poor blackfellow,
All you ever had
Was ancestor Biami,
Except the big bad
Bunyip and his bellow!

DARK MAN

White fellow, true
You had more for pride:
You had Jesus Christ,
But Him you crucified,
And still do.

THE PROTECTORS

While many despise and would exploit us
There are good white men will help us,
But not the appointed and paid officials,
Not the feudal police Protectors,
The protectors who do not protect.

The police of the little far inland towns,
The Protectors of Aborigines
Who move us about at will like cattle
At the request of graziers and their wives:
We feel like owned animals of the Sergeant,
The protector who does not protect.

Is there rape of dark girl by white man or men?
There is no question even of inquiry;
There is no remedy, there is no appeal.
Whom can we appeal to but the Protector
Who feels only contempt for the blacks?
The feeling is mutual, Sergeant!

He sees dark children left without schooling,
Women working from dawn to dark,
        trapped and unhappy;
He jokes with the rest about storekeepers
        robbing the blacks,
He is content with all this,
The little local overlord with all power over us,
The protector who does not protect.

When the white glug contemptuously
Says 'nigger', it is plain to me
He is of lower grade than we.

When the dark stockman, used to hate,
Is not accepted as a mate,
Democracy is empty prate.

When we hear from the white élite
'We won't have abos in our street,'
Their Christianity's a cheat.

When blacks are banned, as we know well,
From city café and hotel,
The stink of Little Rock we smell.

Dark children coming home in tears,
Hurt and bewildered by their jeers —
I think Christ weeps with you, my dears.

People who say, by bias driven,
That colour must not be forgiven,
Would snub the Carpenter in heaven.

BWALLA THE HUNTER

In the hard famine time, in the long drought
Bwalla the hunter on walkabout,
Lubra and children following slow,
All proper hungry long time now.

No more kangaroo out on the plain,
Gone to other country where there was rain.
Couldn't find emu, couldn't find seed,
And the children all time cry for feed.

They saw great eagle come through the sky
To his big stick gunya in a gum near by,
Fine young wallaby carried in his feet:
He bring tucker for his kids to eat.

Big fella eagle circled slow,
Little fella eagles fed below.
'Gwa!' said Bwalla the hunter, 'he
Best fella hunter, better than me.'

He dropped his boomerang. 'Now I climb,
All share tucker in the hungry time.
We got younks too, we got need —
You make fire and we all have feed.'

Then up went Bwalla like a native cat,
All the blackfellows climb like that.
And when he look over big nest rim
Those young ones all sing out at him.

They flapped and spat, they snapped and clawed,
They plenty wild with him, my word,
They shrilled at tucker-thief big and brown,
But Bwalla took wallaby and then climbed down.

At the happy chattering evening meal
Nona the lithe and lovely,
Liked by all,
Came out of her mother's gunya,
Naked like the rest, and like the rest
Unconscious of her body
As the dingo pup rolling about in play.
All eyes turned, men and women, all
Had smiles for Nona.
And what did the women see? They saw
The white hand-band above her forehead,
The gay little feather-tuft in her hair
Fixed with gum, and how she wore it.
They saw the necklet of red berries
And the plaited and painted reed arm-band
Jarri had made her.
And what did the men see? Ah, the men.
They did not see armlet or band
Or the bright little feather-tuft in her hair.
They had no eye for the red berries,
They did not look at these things at all.

No more boomerang
No more spear;
Now all civilized —
Colour bar and beer.

No more corroboree,
Gay dance and din.
Now we got movies,
And pay to go in.

No more sharing
What the hunter brings.
Now we work for money,
Then pay it back for things.

Now we track bosses
To catch a few bob,
Now we go walkabout
On bus to the job.

One time naked,
Who never knew shame;
Now we put clothes on
To hide whatsaname.

No more gunya,
Now bungalow,

Paid by hire purchase
In twenty year or so.

Lay down the stone axe,
Take up the steel,
And work like a nigger
For a white man meal.

No more firesticks
That made the whites scoff.
Now all electric,
And no better off.

Bunyip he finish,
Now got instead
White fella Bunyip,
Call him Red.

Abstract picture now —
What they coming at?
Cripes, in our caves we
Did better than that.

Black hunted wallaby,
White hunt dollar;
White fella witch-doctor
Wear dog-collar.

No more message-stick;
Lubras and lads
Got television now,
Mostly ads.

Lay down the woomera,
Lay down the waddy.
Now we got atom-bomb,
End *every*body.

Stone Age youth
Impatient for the testing
Waits command of elders
To face Bora ordeal.
Boyhood is over,
No more now
Playing with the children,
Keeping with the women;
Today at the Bora
Terrified but eager
Boy becomes man.

He will not dare
To cry when the stone knife
Shapes bleeding Bora marks
Of manhood and honour.
Deep scorn and anger
Should he fail the man test.

He will be given now
Woomera and firesticks,
Given balanced boomerang,
War shield and spear.
He will be tracker now
A tribesman, a fighter,

Sitting with the men now,
Dancing in corroboree;
Going with the hunters
To prove himself a man.

Proudly he'll return now
From his first stalking,
Flinging down his weapons,
Flinging down the kill.
The children he played with
See a boy no longer,
He who passed the Bora,
He who bears a man's marks,
He who knows what men know,
All the tribal secrets.

Now as man Bora-made
He has right to lubra.
With eyes shy and shining
She whom he is given
Peeps through her fingers:
This is her man.
Glad she will follow him,
Wait upon her man's word,
Care for his every need,

In their own gunya
Proud to be his woman,
Proud of her man.

We want hope, not racialism,
Brotherhood, not ostracism,
Black advance, not white ascendance:
Make us equals, not dependants.
We need help, not exploitation,
We want freedom, not frustration;
Not control, but self-reliance,
Independence, not compliance,
Not rebuff, but education,
Self-respect, not resignation.
Free us from a mean subjection,
From a bureaucrat Protection.
Let's forget the old-time slavers:
Give us fellowship, not favours;
Encouragement, not prohibitions,
Homes, not settlements and missions.
We need love, not overlordship,
Grip of hand, not whip-hand wardship;
Opportunity that places
White and black on equal basis.
You dishearten, not defend us,
Circumscribe, who should befriend us.
Give us welcome, not aversion,
Give us choice, not cold coercion,
Status, not discrimination,

Human rights, not segregation.
You the law, like Roman Pontius,
Make us proud, not colour-conscious;
Give the deal you still deny us,
Give goodwill, not bigot bias;
Give ambition, not prevention,
Confidence, not condescension;
Give incentive, not restriction,
Give us Christ, not crucifixion.
Though baptized and blessed and Bibled
We are still tabooed and libelled.
You devout Salvation-sellers,
Make us neighbours, not fringe-dwellers;
Make us mates, not poor relations,
Citizens, not serfs on stations.
Must we native Old Australians
In our land rank as aliens?
Banish bans and conquer caste,
Then we'll win our own at last.

Note: This poem was prepared for and presented to the 5th
Annual General Meeting of the Federal Council for the
Advancement of Aborigines and Torres Strait Islanders, held
in Adelaide, Easter 1962.

We are the food gatherers, we
And all the busy lives we see,
Fur and feathers, the large and small,
With Nature's plenty for us all:
The hawk circling over the plains,
The dingo, scourge of his domains,
The lone owl whose voice forlorn
Pursues the sunset into dawn.
Even the small bronze chickowee
That gossips in bright melody —
Look, into the clump he's gone,
He has a little murder on!
For food is life and life is still
The old carnage, and all must kill
Others, though why wise Nature planned
Red rapine, who can understand?
Only for food, never for sport,
That new evil the white man brought.
Lovely to see them day by day,
The food gatherers, busy and gay,
But most of all we love our own,
When as the dulled red sun goes down
Fishers and hunters home return
To where the family fires burn.

Food now and merriment,
Bellies full and all content,
Around the fires at wide nightfall,
This the happiest time of all.

GIFTS

'I will bring you love,' said the young lover,
'A glad light to dance in your dark eye.
Pendants I will bring of the white bone,
And gay parrot feathers to deck your hair.'

But she only shook her head.

'I will put a child in your arms,' he said,
'Will be a great headman, great rain-maker.
I will make remembered songs about you
That all the tribes in all the wandering camps
Will sing for ever.'

But she was not impressed.

'I will bring you the still moonlight on the lagoon,
And steal for you the singing of all the birds;
I will bring down the stars of heaven to you,
And put the bright rainbow into your hand.'

'No,' she said, 'bring me tree-grubs.'

A SONG OF HOPE

Look up, my people,
The dawn is breaking,
The world is waking
   To a new bright day,
When none defame us,
No restriction tame us,
Nor colour shame us,
   Nor sneer dismay.

Now brood no more
On the years behind you,
The hope assigned you
   Shall the past replace,
When a juster justice
Grown wise and stronger
Points the bone no longer
   At a darker race.

So long we waited
Bound and frustrated,
Till hate be hated
   And caste deposed;
Now light shall guide us,
No goal denied us,
And all doors open
   That long were closed.

See plain the promise,
Dark freedom-lover!
Night's nearly over,
    And though long the climb,
New rights will greet us,
New mateship meet us,
And joy complete us
    In our new Dream Time.

To our fathers' fathers
    The pain, the sorrow;
To our children's children
    The glad tomorrow.

Racism:
Destroy it?
How?
The monster
lives
because
It was created
Strong
With white iron will.
Created
To control
Black.
White monster
Uncontrolled
Controls
The maker.
Soon the monster maker
Will die.
A black black monster
With black iron will
Will live
And become master.

Created for the purpose
Of spinning
Wheels
  in wheels
    in wheels.

Bhoori the hunter left the hill,
For now the western sky was red,
And all the world grew sad and still.

The trees whispered as he went by.
It was a lonely place. He heard
The crake cry and the plover cry.

He stopped and stared. There in the green
A strange woman stood watching him,
The loveliest he had ever seen.

She turned and ran a little way,
Then waited, looking back at him.
'Follow, follow,' she seemed to say.

'Oh, I must follow her,' said he.
'She will be in my dreams for ever
If now I let her go from me.'

Again she ran, again she stayed,
And ever led and lured him on
Half eagerly and half afraid,

Until a water barred the way,
The hushed swamp of the Woor Woman
Where none would venture night or day.

Beyond he saw the water gleam.
'Follow, follow,' she seemed to say.
Bhoori followed as one in dream.

Then out upon the water dim
Lightly she ran and there stood,
Stood on the water watching him.

'Now I have seen it, now I know
She is of the Shadow People.'

And when like friendly comfort came
The red camp fires of his tribe
They welcomed him and called his name.

But Bhoori seemed as one in thrall,
For these to him were now strangers,
Faces he did not know at all.

They heard his tale all wonder-eyed,
And some smiled, but the old men
Shook their heads and talked aside.

'It is the sign of old,' they said.
'Bhoori has seen the Woor Woman,
In three days' time we'll find him dead.'

Dark brothers, first Australian race,
Soon you will take your rightful place
In the brotherhood long waited for,
    Fringe-dwellers no more.

Sore, sore the tears you shed
When hope seemed folly and justice dead.
Was the long night weary? Look up, dark band,
    The dawn is at hand.

Go forward proudly and unafraid
To your birthright all too long delayed,
For soon now the shame of the past
    Will be over at last.

You will be welcomed mateship-wise
In industry and in enterprise;
No profession will bar the door,
    Fringe-dwellers no more.

Dark and white upon common ground
In club and office and social round,
Yours the feel of a friendly land,
    The grip of the hand.

Sharing the same equality
In college and university,
All ambitions of hand or brain
  Yours to attain.

For ban and bias will soon be gone,
The future beckons you bravely on
To art and letters and nation lore,
  Fringe-dwellers no more.

MUNICIPAL GUM

Gumtree in the city street,
Hard bitumen around your feet,
Rather you should be
In the cool world of leafy forest halls
And wild bird calls.
Here you seem to me
Like that poor cart-horse
Castrated, broken, a thing wronged,
Strapped and buckled, its hell prolonged,
Whose hung head and listless mien express
Its hopelessness.
Municipal gum, it is dolorous
To see you thus
Set in your black grass of bitumen —
O fellow citizen,
What have they done to us?

Possess me? No, I cannot give
   The love that others know,
For I am wedded to a cause:
   The rest I must forgo.

You claim me as your very own,
   My body, soul and mind;
My love is my own people first,
   And after that, mankind.

The social part, the personal
   I have renounced of old;
Mine is a dedicated life,
   No man's to have and hold.

Old white intolerance hems me round,
   Insult and scorn assail;
I must be free, I must be strong
   To fight and not to fail.

For there are ancient wrongs to right,
   Men's malice to endure;
A long road and a lonely road,
   But oh, the goal is sure.

When vile men jeer because my skin is brown,
This I live down.

But when a taunted child comes home in tears,
Fierce anger sears.

The colour bar! It shows the meaner mind
Of moron kind.

Men are but medieval yet, as long
As lives this wrong.

Could he but see, the colour-baiting clod
Is blaming God

Who made us all, and all His children He
Loves equally.

As long as brothers banned from brotherhood
You still exclude,

The Christianity you hold so high
Is but a lie,

Justice a cant of hypocrites, content
With precedent.

Gone the gay laughter of the old happy days,
And all because of Boola and his arrogant ways,
Who broke the good camp code
　　　　that each tribe obeys.

Leader in the skill games
　　　　with boomerang and spear,
Ever ready with a scowl, ready with a jeer,
Boola loved to dominate, loved to domineer.

For Boola the masterful scorned the old and wise
With his truculent questions and truculent replies;
Even the wise headman he dared to criticize.

He took married lubras
　　　　and there was nothing said,
For he was quick to give a blow,
　　　　he was held in dread.
They feared the wife-stealer so
　　　　they beat the wives instead.

When the great drought continued
　　　　they knew what caused the ill:
Some wizard of a far tribe working his evil will,
And they must send a death-band
　　　　to seek him out and kill.

They called a men's council, but he did not obey.
'Old men all yabba-yabba.' For Boola every day
Was scornful of the elders, and went his own way.

Out at the council talk-place the conference began
To settle who was guilty
        and make the vengeance plan.
'It could be that Boola,'
        growled Darg the witch-man.

Then quick eyes met other eyes,
        and each one knew
The thinking of his neighbour,
        and the silence grew.
'That fellow plenty bad,' agreed an old pinnaroo.

The grey headman spoke to them:
        'Gather close about,
We will hold the spirit rites, we will find out.
Let Darg do his magic to see
        who made the drought.'

They pressed close to watch it,
        absorbed by the spell
Of the witch-doctor's magic,
        but now they knew well

How dark omens would be read
        and what the signs would tell.

When suddenly the fierce band burst
        on the camp near by
The women screamed,
        the dogs fled as spears began to fly,
And frantic Boola saw too late
        he was the one to die.

A camp moves when death comes,
        and they made haste to go,
No wailing for dead Boola,
        no tree-grave would he know;
They left him on the ground
        there for carrion kite and crow.

ARTIST SON

To Kabul of the tribe Noonuccal (Vivian Walker)

My artist son,
Busy with brush, absorbed in more than play,
Untutored yet, striving alone to find
What colour and form can say,
Yours the deep human need,
The old compulsion, ever since man had mind
And learned to dream,
Adventuring, creative, unconfined.
Even in dim beginning days,
Long before written word was known,
Your fathers too fashioned their art
Who had but bark and wood and the cave stone.
Much you must learn from others, yes,
But copy none; follow no fashions, know
Art the adventurer his lone way
Lonely must go.
Paint joy, not pain,
Paint beauty and happiness for men,
Paint the rare insight glimpses that express
What tongue cannot or pen;
Not for reward, acclaim
That wins honour and opens doors,
Not as ambition toils for fame,
But as the lark sings and the eagle soars.

Make us songs in colour and line:
Painting is speech, painter and poet are one.
Paint what you feel more than the thing you see,
My artist son.

SON OF MINE

To Denis

My son, your troubled eyes search mine,
Puzzled and hurt by colour line.
Your black skin soft as velvet shine;
What can I tell you, son of mine?

I could tell you of heartbreak, hatred blind,
I could tell of crimes that shame mankind,
Of brutal wrong and deeds malign,
Of rape and murder, son of mine;

But I'll tell instead of brave and fine
When lives of black and white entwine,
And men in brotherhood combine —
This would I tell you, son of mine.

I dare not live too long
Life may last for ever.
In a span of life
Ten million lives are lost
And few are found.

Dead men roam
The streets
Screaming obscenities,
Cursing, damning.
Forcing me to look
At my dead life
And theirs.

Hello tree;
Talk to me.
I'm sick
And lonely.

Are you old?
Trunk so cold.
What secrets
Do you hold?

Talk tree!
Can't you see;
My troubles
Trouble me.

Silent tree
Let me see
Your answers.
ANSWER ME.

Tree!
You dare
Question ME?
How dare you
Dare, question ME.

Outside his new-made gunya Jarri
With a sudden howl started to make a song.
He had something to sing about, he
Had been given the pretty Nona,
He was making a song about Nona.
Jarri never made song to remember
But many times he made camp laugh.
Now they laughed at Jarri's love song,
They all liked that cheerful fellow, all
But sour old Yundi.
Jarri sat with legs out
Thudding a hollow log with waddy
To make rhythm, he raised voice
To the yelling chant of the good song-men
Nona laughed with them, proud of Jarri,
Happy to share all eyes with Jarri.
Only old Yundi scowled.
And this the love song Jarri sang them:

I got belly-bruise from a club,
But I . . . got . . . Nona!
I got a sore where I sit down
But I . . . got . . . Nona.
Lost 'em firesticks, broke it woomera.
No more fishnet, no more tomahawk,

Got no gooreen, got no shield,
But I . . . got . . . Nona.

Gootchi he got bark canoe
But I . . . got . . . Nona.
Yarrawan sleep with hunting-dog
But I got Nona.
Kaa got pitcheri, Gwabba got drone-pipe,
Mullawa he got three boomerangs and two
dingoes,
Walla got possum-rug keep him warm,
But I . . . got . . . Nona.

Gecko fella, he got two tails,
But I . . . got . . . Nona.
Frog he only got other frog
But I . . . got . . . Nona.
Gwoon got Weela with big hind part,
She got seven kids before he start,
Grey old Yundi got withered old Yan,
But I . . . got . . . Nona.

Note: Gooreen, a heavy throwing-stick used in hunting. *Pitcheri (pituri)*, a native plant gathered and chewed by some tribes for its narcotic properties. The little gecko lizard seen on tree trunks easily sheds its tail when seized, and this often saves its life. The tail grows again but the new growth is often abnormal, and geckoes with double tails are to be seen.

COMMUNITY RAIN SONG

At the old tribal squatting-place
Behind the camp gunyas
Tonight they were doing their Wyambi rain song
Under the bright stars.
This was nardoo-gathering season
But now little nardoo. Too long dry,
Grass all brown, birds not breeding,
Creeks not running, clouds gone long time.
This not a ritual secret and sacred,
This a camp game, a community playabout,
Even the women there, even the children.
But some of the old men, aloof and grave
Throughout all the laughter muttered strange
    words
Of magic-making as old as the race,
Handed down through countless generations,
Not understood now but faithfully repeated,
Lost rain-words from ancestral times.
Behind the bushes sounded
The weird whirring drone of the dread bullroarer,
While all waited motionless
As a great figure-group carved in stone
Dim in the firelight.

Now into view with dance steps advancing

A line of painted song-men
Chanting in Unison:
'*Rain come down!*
Rain come down!'
And the squatting horde in chorus:
'Rain come down!'
'*Creek run soon!*
Creek run soon!
You great sky ones, fill dry waterhole,
Send rain down!'
'Creek run soon!
Send rain down!'
'*Rainbird come,*
That fellow know, he talk and tell us
Rain fall down!'
At once the whole Wyambi people
Took up the loud toneless scream
Of the giant cuckoo they called the rainbird

Whose coming always predicted rain.
A rhythm of 'Rain fall down!' mingled
With the harsh calls of the bird.

'*Frog talk now,*
Wake up now,

Frog fellow singing out, they telling all about
Rain come down!'
Joyously then the tribe came in
With the croaking of frogs little and big,
Filling a swamp with bedlam of joy
At the nearness of rain:
'Wark, awark, wark!'
'Eek, eek, cree-eek!'
'Ork! Ork!'

'*Plover here now,*
Plover loud now,
He sure rain-bringer, he tell blackfellow
Rain fall down!'
From all the rows of people now
Came perfectly the spurwinged plover's sharp
Excited staccato:
'Karra-karak!'
'Keerk-keerk!'
'Karaka-karra-karak!'

'*Wind he come,*
Little wind first time,
He say soon big blow follow him
And rain fall down!'

'Weẹ-oo, whoo-oo!' came the wail of the wind,
'Whish-awhee-ee!'
'Awhoo-whoo!'

'Thunder up there,
Rumble up there,
Dooloomai the Thunderer he tumble all about,
Shake rain down!'
Like answer came a deep rolling thunder
From the men, while the women with open palms
Beat rapidly upon skin rugs

Stretched taut between their knees like drums
Till the hollow sound
Swelled to a loud booming and then
Gradually died away.

'Rain come down! Rain come down!'
Chorused the line of dancers, threw
In the air handfuls of water
From bark yorlis as they stamped and swayed,
Chanting
The repetitions of the rain song,
While from the ranked Wyambis rose
The toneless monotone of showers,

Hard to do and done superbly —
Leafy boughs, rattling gravel, voices, all
Blended as one to reproduce
The universal sound of steady rain.

The tempo increased, all the rain symbols now
Mingled in pandemonium. Frogs croaked,
Rainbird screamed, thunder rolled,
The rising whine of wind
Cut across cries of plover, and
As background to it all
The deep steady drumming of the rain:
'Wark, awark-wark!'
'Wee-whoo-awhoo!'
'Karra-karak-karak!'
'Boom! Bombomba-oom-m-m!'
'Cree-eek! Ork! Ork!'
'Whish-awhee-ee!'
'Rain come down! Rain come down!'
It looked like going on half the night.
A dingo on a low ridge
Half a mile away
Stood motionless with pricked ears looking down
On the strange goings-on below, dim-lit

By the dying Wyambi fires. These
Were the feared and hated men-creatures
Nothing in all the bush could understand.
He turned away into the dark.

Down on the squatting-place,
Lost in the merry-making, no one marked
The rising of a little wind
That rustled the belahs and then began
To sway them; none saw
That the clear stars above them had disappeared.
Suddenly
A blinding white fork of lightning
Stood for an instant close above them
And instantaneously
A double shattering crash of thunder
That shook the world. All sprang up
Laughing and screaming,
Half in terror and half in joy as the first
Slow drops of rain began to fall; the wind
Whipped up to a gale and whooped about them,
Sparks from the fires
Went whirled in showers across the dark
As the rain roared to a downpour.

'The caves! The caves!'
Some snatched up firesticks and in a straggling line
The excited Wyambi people
Went streaming off along the empty creek
Towards the great red caves of sandstone where
They sheltered at night in the worst wet weather.
Oi! Oi! Good playabout that time!
Oi! Oi! A night to be remembered.

Aboriginal man, you walked with pride,
And painted with joy the countryside.
Original man, your fame grew fast,
Men pointed you out as you went past.

But vain the honour and tributes paid,
For you strangled in rules the white men made;
You broke no law of your own wild clan
Which says, 'Share all with your fellow-man.'

What did their loud acclaim avail
Who gave you honour, then gave you jail?
Namatjira, they boomed your art,
They called you genius, then broke your heart.

THE DISPOSSESSED

For Uncle Willie McKenzie

Peace was yours, Australian man,
    with tribal laws you made,
Till white Colonials stole your peace
    with rape and murder raid;
They shot and poisoned and enslaved
    until, a scattered few,
Only a remnant now remain,
    and the heart dies in you.
The white man claimed your hunting grounds
    and you could not remain,
They made you work as menials
    for greedy private gain;
Your tribes are broken vagrants now
    wherever whites abide,
And justice of the white man
    means justice to you denied.
They brought you Bibles and disease,
    the liquor and the gun:
With Christian culture such as these
    the white command was won.
A dying race you linger on,
    degraded and oppressed,

Outcasts in your own native land,
　　　you are the dispossessed.

When Churches mean a way of life,
　　　as Christians proudly claim,
And when hypocrisy is scorned
　　　and hate is counted shame,
Then only shall intolerance die
　　　and old injustice cease,
And white and dark as brothers find
　　　equality and peace.
But oh, so long the wait has been,
　　　so slow the justice due,
Courage decays for want of hope,
　　　and the heart dies in you.

Their conversation arrested me. There I was, turned off, relaxing on a garden chair, watching early night swallow the last of the daylight.

In the dusk, two forms came into focus. One was shaking his head and his long hair and beard were outlined against the fading light. He was wearing a long gown. He was telling the other shade where he came from. The other shadow had a beard too. They both looked like socially deprived dropouts. One even poorer than the other. He was naked.

Their skins were dark like they must have got an over-exposure of sun. One was dark dark and the other sort of not-so-dark dark.

The not-so-dark darkie was talking and using his hands to make a point. The other dark darkie noticed the holes in the palms of his hands and asked him, how come.

The not-so-dark darkie dropped his hands and frowned, as though he wasn't sure he should tell the dark darkie his story.

He mentioned something about a cause and a betrayal, but as it happened so long ago he'd just sooner forget it.

The dark darkie said he thought nailing people to bits of wood a bit too crude for him. In his neck of the wood, they killed a man quick and clean. Torture like that wasn't their cup of tea.

The not-so-dark darkie said he didn't hold any grudge in spite of what they had done. The dark darkie said he sounded like a hippie-crit. If his gang had of done that to him, he would have returned in spirit form and put the fear of christ into them all.

The not-so-dark darkie replied he didn't have to, they did just that to themselves. He often heard them saying things like for christ sake, or christ almighty, etcetera, etcetera.

Then he explained to the dark darkie that after they had tortured him to death, they renamed him. Dark darkie asks why. He replied christ knows, that was what sent the cult haywire in the first place.

Everyone wanted to get in on the act. Each generation trying to outsmart the last. Trying to build a bigger and bigger hippie-critter movement. The greedy ones finally got the power away from the others and they used his image as a morale booster and bogey man. Sometimes he was even called the hero of the movement. Then he went on to explain the counter revolutionists within the movement. All races setting up their own particular brand of the movement and trying to run the show.

During the breakaway, they decided to rename him. Now the movement was in such a hell of a mess, he regretted ever starting it. Now togetherness is obsolete as far as they are concerned.

The dark darkie said he felt sorry for him. He sure was a troubled soul. He was glad he did not have that on his plate. Probably because he didn't complicate matters in the first place like the not-so-dark darkie had done. He explained his job was offsiding to a female serpent and he and his gang had the job of spreading peace and love around. He admitted he too had trouble getting his scattered gangs together again, since the christian invaders had come and torn the guts out of them.

The not-so-dark darkie explained he had ideas of peace and love too. Every time they slapped him he turned the other cheek and before he knew it they had him nailed.

The dark darkie shakes his head, looks up at the rain clouds above and says he's overspent his time and that he'd better get back to Shadow Land before closing. Said he'd enjoyed talking to a hippie-critter.

The not-so-dark darkie lifts up his holey hands and says, same here, and to hell with them all, he'd let them carry their own crosses from now on. He was becoming allergic to crosses.

Suddenly a clap of thunder and down came the rain. The two shadows hit the dust and I ran up the stairs, into the light.

Understand, old one,
I mean no desecration
Staring here with the learned ones
At your opened grave.
Now after hundreds of years gone
The men of science coming with
     spade and knowledge
Peer and probe, handle the yellow bones,
To them specimens, to me
More. Deeply moved am I.

Understand, old one,
I mean no lack of reverence.
It is with love
I think of you so long ago laid here
With tears and wailing.
Strongly I feel your presence very near
Haunting the old spot, watching
As we disturb your bones. Poor ghost,
I know, I know you will understand.

What if you came back now
To our new world, the city roaring
There on the old peaceful camping place
Of your red fires along the quiet water,

How you would wonder
At towering stone gunyas high in air
Immense, incredible;
Planes in the sky over, swarms of cars
Like things frantic in flight.
What if you came at night upon these miles
Of clustered neon lights of all colours
Like Christian newly come to his Heaven or Hell
And your own people gone?
Old one of the long ago,
So many generations lie between us
But cannot estrange. Your duty to your race
Was with the simple past, mine
Lies in the present and the coming days.

Note: This came after I had visited an old native burial ground
not far from Brisbane, where University people were excavat-
ing bones and had invited me along. I wrote it down at once
while impressions were still fresh.

You keep quiet now, little fella,
You want big-big Bunyip get you?
You look out, no good this place.
You see that waterhole over there?
He Gooboora, Silent Pool.
Suppose-it you go close up one time
Big fella woor, he wait there,
Big fella Bunyip sit down there,
In Silent Pool many bones down there.
He come up when it is dark,
He belong the big dark, that one.
Don't go away from camp fire, you.
Better you curl up in the gunya,
Go to sleep now, little fella,
Tonight he hungry, hear him roar,
He frighten us, the terrible woor,
He the secret thing, he Fear,
He something we don't know.
Go to sleep now, little fella,
Curl up with the yella dingo.

GOOBOORA, THE SILENT POOL

For Grannie Sunflower, Last of the Noonuccals

Gooboora, Gooboora, the Water of Fear
That awed the Noonuccals once numerous here,
The Bunyip is gone from your bone-strewn bed,
And the clans departed to drift with the dead.

Once in the far time before the whites came
How light were their hearts in the dance and the
    game!
Gooboora, Gooboora, to think that today
A whole happy tribe are all vanished away!

What mystery lurks by the Water of Fear,
And what is the secret still lingering here?
For birds hasten by as in days of old,
No wild thing will drink of your waters cold.

Gooboora, Gooboora, still here you remain,
But where are my people I look for in vain?
They are gone from the hill, they are gone from the
    shore,
And the place of the Silent Pool knows them no
more.

But I think they still gather when daylight is done
And stand round the pool at the setting of sun,
A shadowy band that is now without care,
Fearing no longer the Thing in its lair.

Old Death has passed by you but took the dark
        throng;
Now lost is the Noonuccal language and song.
Gooboora, Gooboora, it makes the heart sore
That you should be here but my people no more!

COOKALINGEE

For Elsie Lewis

Cookalingee, now all day
Station cook in white man's way,
Dressed and fed, provided for,
Sees outside her kitchen door
Ragged band of her own race,
Hungry nomads, black of face.
Never begging, they stand by,
Silent, waiting, wild and shy,
For they know that in their need
Cookalingee gives them feed.
Peeping in, their deep dark eyes
Stare at stove with wide surprise,
Pots and pans and kitchen-ware,
All the white-man wonders there.

Cookalingee, lubra still
Spite of white-man station drill,
Knows the tribal laws of old:
'Share with others what you hold;'
Hears the age-old racial call:
'What we have belongs to all.'
Now she gives with generous hand
White man tucker to that band,
Full tin plate and pannikin
To each hunter, child and gin.

Joyful, on the ground they sit,
With only hands for eating it.
Then upon their way they fare,
Bellies full and no more care.

Cookalingee, lubra still,
Feels her dark eyes softly fill,
Watching as they go content,
Natural as nature meant.
And for all her place and pay
Is she happy now as they?

Wistfully she muses on
Something bartered, something gone.
Songs of old remembered days,
The walkabout, the old free ways.
Blessed with everything she prized,
Trained and safe and civilized,
Much she has that they have not,
but is hers the happier lot?

Lonely in her paradise
Cookalingee sits and cries.

WE ARE GOING

For Grannie Coolwell

They came into the little town
A semi-naked band subdued and silent,
All that remained of their tribe.
They came here to the place
            of their old bora ground
Where now the many white men
            hurry about like ants.
Notice of estate agent reads:
            'Rubbish May Be Tipped Here'.
Now it half covers the traces of the old bora ring.
They sit and are confused,
            they cannot say their thoughts:
'We are as strangers here now,
            but the white tribe are the strangers.
We belong here, we are of the old ways.
We are the corroboree and the bora ground,
We are the old sacred ceremonies,
            the laws of the elders.
We are the wonder tales of Dream Time,
            the tribal legends told.
We are the past, the hunts and the laughing
            games,
            the wandering camp fires.
We are the lightning-bolt over Gaphembah Hill

Quick and terrible,
And the Thunder after him, that loud fellow.
We are the quiet daybreak paling the dark lagoon.
We are the shadow-ghosts creeping back as the
camp fires burn low.
We are nature and the past, all the old ways
Gone now and scattered.
The scrubs are gone, the hunting and the laughter.
The eagle is gone, the emu and the kangaroo are
gone from this place.
The bora ring is gone.
The corroboree is gone.
And we are going.'

UNITED WE WIN

The glare of a thousand years is shed
       on the black man's wistful face,
Fringe-dweller now on the edge of towns,
       one of a dying race;
But he has no bitterness in his heart
       for the white man just the same;
He knows he has white men friends today,
       he knows they are not to blame.
Curse no more the nation's great,
       the glorious pioneers,
Murderers honoured with fame and wealth,
       won of our blood and tears;
Brood no more on the bloody past
       that is gone without regret,
But look to the light of happier days
       that will shine for your children yet.
For in spite of public apathy
       and the segregation pack
There is mateship now,
       and the good white hand
       stretched out to grip the black.
He knows there are white friends here today
       who will help us fight the past,
Till a world of workers from shore to shore as
equals live at last.

SONG

Life is ours in vain
Lacking love, which never
Counts the loss or gain.
But remember, ever
Love is linked with pain.

Light and sister shade
Shape each mortal morrow
Seek not to evade
Love's companion Sorrow,
And be not dismayed.

Grief is not in vain,
It's for our completeness.
If the fates ordain
Love to bring life sweetness,
Welcome too its pain.

GOD'S ONE MISTAKE

It repenteth me that I have made man. — Genesis, 6

I who am ignorant and know so little,
So little of life and less of God,
This I do know
That happiness is intended and could be,
That all wild simple things have life fulfilled
Save man,
That all on earth have natural happiness
Save man.
Without books or schools, lore or philosophy
In my own heart I know
That hate is wrong,
Injustice evil.
Pain there must be and tears,
Sorrow and death, but not
Intolerance, unkindness, cruelty,
Unless men choose
The mean and base, which Nature never made,
But we alone.
And sometimes I will think that God looks down
With loving smile, saying,
'Poor child, poor child, maybe I was wrong
In planning for you reason and free will
To fashion your own life in your own way.
for all the rest
I settled and appointed as for children

Their simple days, but you
I gave the Godlike gift to choose,
Who were not wise — for see how you have
chosen,
Poor child, alone among them all now
Unhappy on the earth.'

I

After all creeds since reason first began,
Though it seems odd,
I'm still uncertain whether God made man
Or man made God.

II

When someone invented the rope
It wasn't so long till some other
Improved its use by inventing the noose,
And we started to hang one another.

III

Appearance is the world's test.
Brother, you're treated as you're dressed.

IV

'Man born of woman is a mess.
Adam alone was perfect man.'
'Aw, I don't know,' piped little Joe,
'He had no belly-button, Gran.'

V

Of all the ways to waste our days

Whose lives are short at best,
Listening to piano solos
Is one of the dreariest.

VI

'Prate not of God whom none has seen,
Poor dupe as credulous as blind.'
Wiseacre who must see to know,
You've never seen your own behind.

VII

Man's endless quest is to be happy,
Ever since Cain wet his first nappy;
Yet crime-waves now and A-bomb plans,
And Yanks turned Schickelgruber fans.

VIII

If Christ returned today among us, he
Once more would meet cold eye of Sadducee,
Security Boys would whisper and insist,
McCarthyites would chorus 'Communist!'

IX

Don't say Sir Boodle Blimp ignores the arts.

For golf his culture is both deep and strong;
Financial columns are his poetry;
His favourite music is the dinner gong.

X

All our lives my brothers, we
Have fought for a just equality.
Patience! At last it will be found:
We are all equal under the ground.

CIVILIZATION

We who came late to civilization,
Missing a gap of centuries,
When you came we marvelled and admired,
But with foreboding.
We had so little but we had happiness,
Each day a holiday,
For we were people before we were citizens,
Before we were ratepayers,
Tenants, customers, employees, parishioners.
How could we understand
White man's gradings, rigid and unquestioned,
Your sacred totems of Lord and Lady,
Highness and Holiness, Eminence, Majesty.
We could not understand
Your strange cult of uniformity,
This mass obedience to clocks, time-tables.
Puzzled, we wondered why
The importance to you, urgent and essential,
Of ties and gloves, shoe-polish, uniforms.
New to us were jails and orphanages,
Rents and taxes, banks and mortgages.
We who had so few things, the prime things,
We had no policemen, lawyers, middlemen,
Brokers, financiers, millionaires.

So they bewildered us, all the new wonders,
Stocks and shares, real estate,
Compound interest, sales and investments.
Oh, we have benefited, we have been lifted
With new knowledge, a new world opened.
Suddenly caught up in white man's ways
Gladly and gratefully we accept,
And this is necessity.
But remember, white man, if life is for happiness,
You too, surely, have much to change.

'Mother, what is that one sea,
Sometimes blue or green or yellow?'
'That Biami's waterhole.
He big fellow.'

'Mother, what make sunset fire,
Every night the big red glare?'
'Biami's gunya out that way,
That his camp fire over there.'

'How come great wide river here,
Where we swim and fish with spear?'
'Biami dug him.
You see big hills all about?
They the stuff that he chuck out.'

Note: Among white people Biami is the best known of the great
Aboriginal Ancestors who made the world and men. They
were not gods, not worshipped, but were highly venerated.

FREEDOM

For Vivian Charles

Brumby on the wide plain,
All men out to break you,
My warm fellow-feeling
Hopes they never take you!

Dingo on the lone ridge,
Fleeing as you spy them,
Every hand against you,
May you still defy them!

All things wild and tameless,
Hunted down and hated,
Something in my wild heart
With your own is mated.

Dingo, wild bushranger,
Brumby that they ban so,
May you still outmatch them,
May you foil the man-foe!

Lover of my happy past
Soothe my weariness
With warm embrace.
Turn not from me,
Communicate.
Am I strayed too long
And now forsaken?
Your cold winds freeze
My offered love.

Was it yesterday
Or a thousand years,
My eager feet
Caressed your paths;
My opened fingers
Counted grains of sand
Hidden in the warmth of time.

Now my civilized self
Stamps its imprint
On reluctant sands
And time has flown.
Impatient to converse
My brutalness
Turns you from my touch —

Oh lost, neglected love,
My tear-stained eyes
Open now to see
Your enemy and mine
Is — civilized me.

As tribal elders sit,
Their tribal thoughts tie their tongue.
We, the foreigners,
In this our land,
Know not
Where lies our future track.
No place forward,
None back.

Hearing their city tribes
Talk the foreign tongue,
They shuffle their tribal feet,
And wait,
And judge,
And soon, within their age-old eyes,
A light appears:
Yes, it was there,
Though but a pinhead size.

Frustrated still
They walk away,
With knowing smile
And gentle voice.
Now . . .
We hope . . .
For you have taught us
. . . hope . . . there is.

RACISM

Stalking the corridors of life,
Black, frustrated minds
Scream for release
From Christian racist moulds.
Moulds that enslave
Black independence.

Take care! white racists!
Blacks can be racists too.
A violent struggle could erupt
And racists meet their death.

Colour, the gift of nature
To mankind,
Is now the contentious bone,
And black-white hatred sustains itself
On the rotting, putrid flesh
That once was man.

I am black of skin among whites,
And I am proud,
Proud of race and proud of skin.
I am broken and poor,
Dressed in rags from white man's back,
But do not think I am ashamed.
Spears could not contend against guns
        and we were mastered,
But there are things they could not plunder and
        destroy.
We were conquered but never subservient,
We were compelled but never servile.
Do not think I cringe as white men cringe to
        whites.
I am proud,
Though humble and poor and without a home . . .
So was Christ.

THEN AND NOW

In my dreams I hear my tribe
Laughing as they hunt and swim,
But dreams are shattered by rushing car,
By grinding tram and hissing train,
And I see no more my tribe of old
As I walk alone in the teeming town.

I have seen corroboree
Where that factory belches smoke;
Here where they have memorial park
One time lubras dug for yams;
One time our dark children played
There where the railway yards are now,
And where I remember the didgeridoo
Calling to us to dance and play,
Offices now, neon lights now,
Bank and shop and advertisement now,
Traffic and trade of the busy town.

No more woomera, no more boomerang,
No more playabout, no more the old ways.
Children of nature we were then,
No clocks hurrying crowds to toil.

Now I am civilized and work in the white way,
Now I have dress, now I have shoes:
'Isn't she lucky to have a good job!'
Better when I had only a dillybag.
Better when I had nothing but happiness.

DAISY BINDI

Slavery at Roy Hill, to our shame profound,
Wages for the blacks nil all the year round,
Slavers given free hand by police consent,
Winked at obligingly by Government.
But a woman warrior where aid there was none
Led her dark people till the fight was won.

> Salute to a spirit fine,
> Daisy of Nullagine,
> Who unaided resolutely
> Dared to challenge slavery.

Tall Daisy Bindi, she rode like a man,
Mustering and stockwork from when dawn began,
And long chores indoors that made life bleak
Year after weary year for nothing a week,
Till Daisy of the stout heart organized her clan
To strike for native justice and
                    the plain rights of man.

> High praise and honour to
> Daisy of the Noongahs who
> Fought and routed tyranny,
> Dared to challenge slavery.

Oh, the boss men threatened
          and the boss men swore,
They called the police in to help break the law,
And dark men and women were forced and
          assailed,
For fighting degradation they were bashed and
          jailed,
But Daisy the militant no man subdued,
Who championed her people out of servitude.

Note: Mrs Daisy Bindi of Western Australia's far inland made
a name for herself as an Aboriginal leader of her people. On
Roy Hill Station where she worked, the native stockmen and
domestics received no wages till at last she organized them and
fought for the rights of her race. It was a long struggle and
marked by disgraceful incidents against the Aborigines con-
cerned, but the final result was victory and the establishment
of the present admirable Pindan Co-operative Aboriginal
community at Port Hedland.

THE PAST

Let no one say the past is dead.
The past is all about us and within.
Haunted by tribal memories, I know
This little now, this accidental present
Is not the all of me, whose long making
Is so much of the past.

Tonight here in suburbia as I sit
In easy chair before electric heater,
Warmed by the red glow, I fall into dream:
I am away
At the camp fire in the bush, among
My own people, sitting on the ground,
No walls about me,
The stars over me,
The tall surrounding trees that stir in the wind
Making their own music,
Soft cries of the night coming to us, there
Where we are one with all old Nature's lives
Known and unknown,
In scenes where we belong but have now forsaken.
Deep chair and electric radiator
Are but since yesterday,

But a thousand thousand camp fires in the forest
Are in my blood.
Let none tell me the past is wholly gone.
Now is so small a part of time, so small a part
Of all the race years that have moulded me.

The miner rapes
The heart of earth
With his violent spade.
Stealing, bottling her black blood
For the sake of greedy trade.
On his metal throne of destruction,
He labours away with a will,
Piling the mountainous minerals high
With giant tool and iron drill.

In his greedy lust for power,
He destroys old nature's will.
For the sake of the filthy dollar,
He dirties the nest he builds.
Well he knows that violence
Of his destructive kind
Will be violently written
Upon the sands of time.

But time is running out
And time is close at hand,
For the Dreamtime folk are massing
To defend their timeless land.

Come gentle black man
Show your strength;
Time to take a stand.
Make the violent miner feel
Your violent
Love of land.

BALANCE

Spin a coin:
Life or death.
Next of kin
To death
Is life,
And life
To death.

Light comes
Before dark.
In life we wait
The birth of death.

BOOKS PUBLISHED BY KATH WALKER IN AUSTRALIA

We Are Going. Jacaranda Wiley. 1964.

The Dawn Is At Hand. Jacaranda Wiley. 1966.

Stradbroke Dreamtime. Angus and Robertson. 1970.

Father Sky and Mother Earth. Jacaranda Wiley. 1981.

My People. Jacaranda Wiley. 1970, revised 1981, 1990.

Australian Legends and Landscapes. Random House Australia. 1990.

FIRST LINE INDEX

BIOGRAPHY

On 3 November 1920, Kathleen Jean Mary Ruska was born on North Stradbroke, an island in Moreton Bay about 30 kilometres east of Brisbane, and the home of the Noonuccal tribe.

There were seven children in the Ruska family, and all spent some time at the Dunwich Primary School. At the age of 13, and as an Aborigine with no future in the State Education System, Kath went into domestic service in Brisbane. She was rescued from that fate by the Second World War when she served in the Australian Women's Army Service.

Kath married Bruce Walker, a waterside worker in Brisbane, and had two sons, Denis and Vivian. She joined the Communist Party because it was the only political organization that eschewed the White Australia Policy, but left it because the Party wanted to write her speeches!

The sixties — the years of freedom rides, the struggle for the right to vote and the Gurindji strike at Wave Hill — saw Kath Walker become a prominent and persuasive figure as she wrote and spoke for Aboriginal Rights, perhaps following the path of her father who had been active in the struggle for award wages for Aborigines as early as 1935.

In 1964 her first volume of verse and the first by an Australian Aborigine, *We Are Going*, was published (with the encouragement of Judith Wright and the aid of a Commonwealth Literary Fund) by The Jacaranda Press, Australia. Her second volume, *The Dawn Is at Hand*, followed in 1966. The honest and outspoken poems gained immediate acceptance and they were to be the forerunners of a considerable output which includes short stories, speeches, paintings, drama and film.

The Civil Rights struggle of the 60s and 70s saw Kath active on many local, State and, later, National Committees. She was Queensland State Secretary of the Federal Council for the Advancement of Aborigines and Torres Strait Islanders, Secretary of the Queensland State Council for the Advancement of Aborigines and Torres Strait Islanders, and a member of the Queensland Aboriginal Advancement League.

During this time of heightened activity associated with pressure to amend Section 51 and repeal Section 127 of the Australian Constitution, Kath Walker was part of the delegation which presented the case for reform to Prime Minister Menzies. This lobbying led to one of the most important Constitutional reforms since Federation when, on 27 May 1967, 90% of the Australian Electorate supported the proposed amendments.

Later she served on the Aboriginal Arts Board, the Aboriginal Housing Committee and was chairperson of the National Tribal Council and the Stradbroke Land

Council. Since 1972 she has been Managing Director of the Noonuccal-Nughie Education Cultural Centre, as well as being a remedial teacher at Dunwich School. She has lectured at universities and colleges throughout Australia on subjects ranging from uranium mining to conservation and the environment to Aboriginal culture.

In 1969 Kath Walker was the Australian delegate to the World Council of Churches Consultation on Racism in London, bringing the plight of her people to overseas attention for the first time.

This was the beginning of many a foray into the world outside Australia. In 1972 she was guest lecturer at the University of the South Pacific in Fiji; in 1974 the official Australian envoy at the International Writers' Conference in Malaysia; in 1975 the guest of the PNG Government at the PNG Festival of Arts; and in 1976 delegate and Senior Advisor to the Second World Black Festival of the Arts held in Lagos, Nigeria (surviving a plane hijack on her way home).

In 1978–9 she won a Fulbright Scholarship and Myer Travel Grant to the United States of America and was Poet-in-Residence at Bloomsburg State College, Pennsylvania.

In these same years, almost as if it were a necessary antidote to travel, she established Moongalba, or 'sitting-down-place', a five-hectare piece of coastal bushland on North Stradbroke Island where archaeological evidence shows that her ancestors had been in occupation for over 20,000 years. There in her caravan she welcomed visitors of all ages and races.

For many Aboriginal and Islander children from the cities, this was their first experience of the natural way of life of their ancestors. For people of other races it was a rare insight into another culture. To date, over 28,000 children and adults have learned about Aboriginal food-gathering practices, participated in a revival of arts and crafts, and listened to Aboriginal story tellers, and by so doing have come to understand, and more particularly respect, the often fragile but sustaining interrelationships of Australian nature.

Kath was the subject of Frank Heiman's film *Shadow Sister* (1977) for which she received an International Acting Award and membership of the Black Hall of Fame. In 1970 the first edition of her anthology *My People* (Jacaranda Press, Australia) was published, and she wrote of her childhood in *Stradbroke Dreamtime* (1972. Angus and Robertson, Australia). As well as being a writer she is also an artist in her own right. She has illustrated her own book (*Father Sky and Mother Earth*, Jacaranda Press, Australia, 1981), and in 1986 a volume of her paintings (*Quandamooka: The Art of Kath Walker*) was edited by Ulli Beier and published by the Aboriginal

Arts Council with Robert Brown and Associates.

The eighties also saw further travel. In 1985 she was a member of the Australia/China Council party which toured China, and poems written on this tour (*Kath Walker in China*) became the first collection written by an Aborigine to be co-published by Australian and Chinese publishing houses and presented in Chinese and English.

In 1986, at the invitation of Secretary-General Gorbachev, she was a delegate to the International Forum for a Nuclear Free World for the Survival of Humanity held in Moscow. On her way home from Russia she lectured in New Delhi on 'Aboriginal Grass Roots Culture'. And somehow in the same year she managed to be both actor and script consultant for Bruce Beresford's film *The Fringe Dwellers*.

The eighties also saw Kath's close involvement with the Land Rights Movement, which culminated in despair when the Federal Labor Government refused to honour its promise to enact National Land Rights Legislation.

So Kath Walker became Oodgeroo of the tribe Noonuccal, custodian of the land Minjerribah. Many of her awards she retained — the Jessie Litchfield Award, the Mary Gilmore Medal, and the Fellowship of Australian Writers' Award. But in 1987, as a Bicentennial protest, she returned the insignia of the MBE (awarded back in 1970) to the Crown via the Governor of Queensland. Notwithstanding this action, Oodgeroo and her son Kabul (Vivian) were scriptwriters and producers for the Dreamtime story, *The Rainbow Serpent*, which was a major feature of the Australian Pavilion at World Expo 88. The text of *The Rainbow Serpent* was subsequently published by the Australian Government Publishing Service.

1988 also was the year of the award of an Honorary Doctor of Letters from Macquarie University.

In 1989 Griffith University awarded her the degree of Doctor of the University, and 1989 saw the world premiere of *The Dawn Is at Hand*, a musical setting of a selection of Oodgeroo's poetry by Malcolm Williamson, an Australian himself and Master of the Queen's Music. This symphonic chorale was performed in Brisbane by the Queensland Symphony Orchestra, soloists and the Queensland State and Municipal Choir.

This volume is her first book in English to be published outside Australia.